Systems of Government

THEOCRACY

Sean Connolly

W
FRANKLIN WATTS
LONDON•SYDNEY

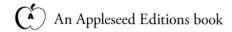 An Appleseed Editions book

First published in 2013 by Franklin Watts
338 Euston Road, London NW1 3BH

Franklin Watts Australia
Hachette Children's Books
Level 17/207 Kent St, Sydney, NSW 2000

© 2012 Appleseed Editions

Created by Appleseed Editions Ltd,
Well House, Friars Hill, Guestling,
East Sussex TN35 4ET

Designed by Hel James
Edited by Mary-Jane Wilkins
Picture research by Su Alexander

ISBN 978 1 4451 0990 9

Dewey Classification 321.5

A CIP catalogue for this book is available from the British Library.

Picture credits
page 5 AFP/Getty Images; 6 Keystone/Getty Images; 9 Daily News L P (New York)/Getty
Images; 10 Stephan Gladieu/Getty Images; 13 &14 Photos.com/Thinkstock; 16 AFP/Getty
Images; 18 Getty Images; 21, 22 & 25 AFP/Getty Images; 26 Time & Life Pictures/Getty
Images; 28 Shutterstock; 30 Donna Day/Getty Images; 33 Zzvet/Shutterstock; 34 Sylvain
Grandadam/Getty Images; 37 Getty Images; 39 ArabianEye/Getty Images; 41 AFP/Getty
Images; 42 Photos.com/Thinkstock; 44 Getty Images

Printed in Malaysia

Franklin Watts is a division of Hachette Children's Books,
an Hachette UK company.
www.hachette.co.uk

Contents

What is a theocracy?

One of the greatest human achievements is the way in which communities of all sizes agree a system of rights and laws which binds them together. People within the community might argue about the exact nature of the rights and laws – as rival candidates do during an election – but they share an overall belief in the system itself.

Their trust is usually placed in organizations (such as a parliament or congress) or in individuals (a prime minister, president or king). Either way, the population agrees that individuals or groups – people like themselves – can shape the way in which they live as a society.

Some societies, however, look beyond their immediate surroundings for guidance on how to live together. If they share a strong religious belief, they might use sacred writings and traditions to guide them in their daily lives. Societies that use religious principles to govern their people are called theocracies. Like the words for some other forms of government (such as **democracy** and autocracy) it is made up of two Greek words. The 'cracy' comes from *kratos*, meaning 'rule' or 'strength'. But it is 'theo' (from *theo,* meaning 'God'), that defines this system.

Combining systems

Other systems of government represent the wishes of all the people through their elected representatives (as in a democracy), or they follow the rule of a powerful individual (as in a **dictatorship**). A theocracy works along different lines. It exists because people want to combine their religious beliefs with their political system.

This book examines how and why theocracies come about, and how well they work as systems of government. It also looks at a number of questions surrounding theocracies, including:
• Do people in theocracies believe the system is fair – and does people's view of fairness matter if they look to God for answers?
• Who decides which version of Christianity, **Islam**, **Buddhism**, or Judaism should take precedence in the community or country?

- Can elements of theocracy coexist with other forms of government?
- Are there likely to be more or fewer theocracies in the future?

The framework of world politics is rapidly changing, and today's answer to that last question is probably different from people's predictions fifteen or fifty years ago.

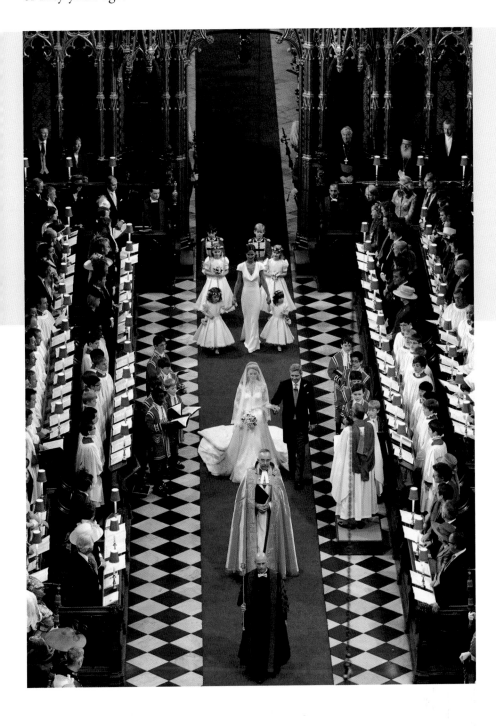

The wedding of Prince William and Catherine Middleton, in London in April 2011. When William becomes king, he will also become supreme governor of the Church of England – a centuries-old merging of Church and state.

Political beliefs

From the earliest times societies have developed different forms of government to impose order and to reflect their shared values. Most of those forms of government have been based on chosen men and women within a society leading it – either by choosing leaders from among themselves or because they accept the leadership of a powerful individual. But in the past, many communities (and even some countries) have allowed their religious beliefs to guide their political life.

MILESTONES IN THEOCRACY

3100 BCE	Northern and southern Egypt unified under one ruler considered divine, served by extensive priesthood
539 BCE	Kingdom of Judah operates as theocracy for six centuries after Jews' return from Babylon
ca CE 70	Jewish historian Flavius Josephus invents term 'theocracy' to distinguish government of the Jews from other types of government
622	Prophet Muhammad establishes Islamic theocracy in Medina
800s–1870	Papal States operate as Catholic theocracy
1260	Kublai Khan converts to Buddhism and approves theocracy in Tibet
1525	Huldrych Zwingli transforms Zurich into theocratic state
1532–1535	Anabaptist theocracy governs German **city-state** of Münster
1554	John Calvin establishes strict **Protestant** theocracy in Geneva
1616	Buddhist theocracy established in Bhutan
1630s	English **Puritans** establish theocratic governments in Massachusetts and Connecticut
1847	**Mormon** settlers establish short-lived state of Deseret in the American West, before Utah becomes an official state
1885–1898	Mahdi defeat British forces and establish Islamic theocracy in Sudan
1905	France passes a law guaranteeing separation of Church and state
1911–1919	Mongolia governed by a Buddhist theocracy
1979	Islamic revolutionaries establish theocratic government in Iran
1996–2001	**Taliban** leaders form Islamic theocracy in Afghanistan

Church and state

Many countries go to great lengths to keep their governments free from religious influence. This attitude is expressed in the phrase 'separating Church (religion) and state (government)'. Choosing to live in a theocracy, or making another type of government more theocratic, means having a completely different view of how people and societies should behave.

Separating Church and state sets clear boundaries between religious-based ideas of right and wrong on the one hand, and legal rules on the other. Countries which cherish freedom of religion – people's right to worship as they choose – also try to make sure that no set of religious beliefs can change the laws of the land. For example, a religion might allow a man to have two or more wives, but in most western countries such **polygamy** is against the law.

A scene from rural Tibet in the 1940s. Tibet was still a Buddhist theocracy when the Chinese invaded and seized control in the 1950s.

RIPE FOR CHANGE?

Fundamentalism is a response to change... which may feed theocratic ideals. The word fundamentalism comes from the fundamental (or basic) beliefs a group shares. A group that feels threatened in some way highly values the search for important shared beliefs. Many religious fundamentalists feel threatened by the pace of change in the modern world. Whether they are Muslims who insist on traditional clothing, Christians who use the Bible to teach science, or Jewish settlers in the Middle East, they look to the past for guidance on how to behave now and in the future.

Fundamentalist views can be very powerful, drawing more people towards them and shaping the direction in which a society – or country – will go in the future.

Being linked to a certain religion can harm politicians' chances in countries with a strong tradition of separating Church from state. John F. Kennedy was Catholic and faced strong opposition from many American voters when he ran for president in 1960. Some people feared that because he was Catholic, Kennedy would allow the ideas of the Pope to influence his decisions as president. Kennedy pointed out that he was running for president not as a Catholic, but as an American, and that people should not be judged politically because of their religious beliefs.

Despite politicians' efforts to keep the state free of Church influence, observers in the US and other western countries have noticed how the two elements collide more and more frequently (see Voice of the People). As more Muslim countries turn to their Islamic faith in political matters, theocratic ideas are alive and well in the twenty-first century.

Back to fundamentals

Today people are accustomed to hearing the word 'fundamentalist' in news stories, often linked to a particular set of religious beliefs. For example, Islamic fundamentalists might stage a protest in Iraq, or Christian fundamentalists in the UK might disagree with a TV series or a subject being taught in schools.

People who believe strongly in fundamentals usually have a cast-iron certainty that their own beliefs are right, and that all opposing beliefs are wrong. This hard-line view is an echo of earlier times, when people went to war over religious differences. It is also a reaction against what many fundamentalists believe were decades of relaxed attitudes in the modern world. As the pace of change has increased, so has the strength of reaction. Will this conflict lead to more theocracies?

A Christian activist holds a placard and cross outside the Supreme Court in Washington, DC in March 2000. He is demonstrating in support of prayer in America's public (or state) schools.

VOICE OF THE PEOPLE

CHURCH AND STATE IN AMERICA
Jean Bethke Elshtain is an expert on the role of religious belief in American society. She believes it is wrong to expect American political life to be free from religious influence. Her words might well apply to other western countries in the future: 'Separation of Church and state is one thing. Separation of religion and politics is something else altogether. Religion and politics flow back and forth in American civil society all the time – always have, always will.'

Is a pure theocracy possible?

It may not be possible to find a society that is a pure theocracy, but the search for an example reveals how often humans have looked beyond themselves for guidance on how to live and be ruled. When we try to identify theocracies, we need to look for societies that have placed their trust in some form of higher being.

A Mormon family photographed in 2008. In the family are one husband and three wives (two of whom are not legally married to the husband) plus 21 children. They are unofficially continuing the early Mormon practice of polygamy.

THE STORY OF DESERET

In 1847 members of the Church of Jesus Christ of the Latter-day Saints (Mormons) established a settlement called Deseret in what is now the state of Utah. Few people lived in this semi-desert area, so the Mormons could be sure that those elected in Deseret supported Mormon principles. The Mormons wanted Deseret to become an American state, but the US government refused to accept some Mormon customs, such as polygamy.

As a Mormon theocracy, Deseret could not become a US **territory** (the first step towards becoming a state). Instead the government reduced its size and called it The Territory of Utah in 1850. Many Mormons were unhappy and continued to obey the laws of the unofficial government calling itself the State of Deseret. They continued to press for a state with purely Mormon principles, but more and more non-Mormons began arriving in Utah, especially after America's first coast-to-coast railway was completed in 1869.

Over the next two decades, Utah began passing laws that took away much of the Mormon church influence. The Mormon church realized it had to **compromise**, and in 1890 it banned polygamy. That removed the last obstacle, and in 1896 Utah officially became a state.

If you study any system of government long enough – today or in the past – you will find it difficult to describe any of them as purely one type of society. Here are some examples.
• The democratic government of ancient Athens: this was democratic in some ways, but many people in Athens could not vote, including women, children, foreigners and slaves.
• The dictatorship in Italy run by Benito Mussolini in the 1930s: during Mussolini's rule people continued to vote democratically in local and regional elections.

• The British **monarchy**: Parliament and other democratic institutions hold the real political power in Britain, so the king or queen is just a symbolic leader.

Necessary compromises?

In each case, what seems to be one type of political system is usually a mixture of two or more. The same holds true with most theocracies, past and present. Some might have had a king or queen; others retain democratic elements. These might dilute the purity of a theocracy, but they might also be necessary compromises.

Why might people living in a theocracy want their government to be less extreme? To answer that, we can look at the type of society that chooses a theocratic form of government, and then see what is needed to retain such a system. A theocracy can only develop when people share religious values and agree about the rules and punishments their beliefs dictate. This sort of society might be hard for modern westerners to imagine, as most western countries allow a huge range of belief (and disbelief) – but there have been long periods of history when people have followed a universally shared religion.

People's everyday lives in ancient Egypt are an example. Their lives revolved around an intricate set of shared beliefs, yet the business of government was run by a strict monarchy, and the pharaoh held great power. In ancient Greece, all Greeks shared traditions associated with their gods, yet the city-states chose either military rule or democracy. The Romans also had a shared religious system, but chose to live under a republic and then an emperor. In the modern world, only Muslim countries come close to operating pure theocracies, but most also have monarchies or some form of representative government.

Experiments with pure theocracy have generally been brief and have been undertaken in a relatively small region. The Swiss city of Geneva governed itself as a Protestant theocracy under the leadership of John Calvin in the sixteenth century. Less than a century later, English Puritans created theocracies in New England, and Mormons in nineteenth-century America established a short-lived theocratic government in a place they called Deseret (see box on page 11).

These systems all faded and the societies were absorbed into wider, non-theocratic governments. But the beliefs behind these pure theocracies remain alive, and many religious people continue to introduce them into modern societies.

Is a pure theocracy possible?

MICHAEL SERVETVS HISPA___S DE ARAGONIA

*The Spanish religious thinker Michael Servetus took the ideas of Martin Luther and John Calvin to new conclusions. His version of Protestant belief was rejected by Calvin's Geneva, and Servetus was burned as a **heretic** in 1553.*

VOICE OF THE PEOPLE

SILENCING A DISSENTING VOICE

*John Calvin was a religious reformer who left his native France and established a theocracy in Geneva. The penalties for those who **dissented** were harsh and delivered swiftly. Here Calvin describes the execution of the Spanish religious reformer Michael Servetus, whose views differed from those of the Geneva theocracy. Servetus was burnt as a heretic on 27 October 1553 on the orders of the Geneva governing council.*

*'Whoever shall maintain that wrong is done to heretics and blasphemers in punishing them makes himself an **accomplice** in their crime and guilty as they are. There is no question here of man's authority; it is God who speaks, and clear it is what law he will have kept in the church, even to the end of the world. Wherefore does he demand of us a so extreme severity, if not to show us that due honour is not paid him, so long as we set not his service above every human consideration, so that we spare not kin, nor blood of any, and forget all humanity when the matter is to combat for His glory.'*

Constitutional systems

As very few pure theocracies exist in today's world, we should look at how religion is still sometimes linked with politics. Church and state might be separate in a country, but how separate are they? Does the **constitution** of a country make special provision for any **denomination**? Theocracy can creep into other forms of government – sometimes in surprising ways.

STATE RELIGIONS

In a number of countries religious denominations are linked in some way to the government. Although most of these countries also cherish the notion of religious freedom, the Church-state link troubles some people. They ask whether it is possible for Church and state to relate to each other in a way that does not allow the Church to dictate laws (as in an outright theocracy) or allow the government to control the actions of the Church.

The government-control approach was common in **communist** countries such as the Soviet Union. There, the government veered between trying to eliminate the Russian Orthodox Church altogether and getting spies to join it so the Church would echo government views. Present-day communist countries adopt a similar policy. Cuba is relatively tolerant of Catholicism and other religious beliefs, but it also organizes 'religious' groups that support the government.

Nowadays, state religion usually means one of two things. The first is a religion – usually a Christian denomination – that most citizens in a country follow. These denominations usually have the country's name in their title. Even though many citizens have drifted away from these churches, they are still linked to the country. Some, such as the Church of England, still maintain an official Church-state link: the reigning monarch is the head of the Church of England. Others, such as the Church of Sweden, have cut official ties with government but (on paper at least) represent most of the citizens.

Islam is another matter. Many Muslims believe that their faith calls for unity across national boundaries, based on shared religion. Although very few Muslim countries can be described as pure theocracies (most have ruling families or representative governments), the religious influence is strong. It can influence many areas, ranging from national laws to foreign policy (see pages 22-25) through education and the media (see pages 38-41).

Henri IV, the French king who became a Catholic to end the nation's religious wars, believed that religious rulers should not dictate every aspect of people's lives.

Schoolgirls in traditional Islamic clothing on their way to class in a Swedish secondary school. Some European countries are struggling to absorb immigrant communities with different religious and social customs.

Europe was torn apart by vicious religious conflict through much of the sixteenth and seventeenth centuries. The conflict was between Catholics and Protestants. For people four or five centuries ago, religion was far more than a matter of conscience. Believers felt that they could save whole populations from eternal damnation if they made sure that people followed the 'true faith' (which varied depending on one's viewpoint). Even in this salvation-or-damnation scenario, Europeans began to accept an idea that would reduce bloodshed.

The idea was summed up in the phrase 'a state follows the religion of its ruler' (in Latin: *cuius regio, eius religio*). The phrase underpinned two important treaties: the Peace of Augsburg (1555), which accepted that most of central Europe was religiously divided, and the Peace of Westphalia (1648), which ended the Thirty Years' War. One outcome was that after 1648 Catholic Spain no longer claimed political (or religious) control over the Protestant Netherlands.

VOICE OF THE PEOPLE

'THE PURE DOCTRINES OF JESUS'

The United States was born in the era known as the Age of **Enlightenment**, when new scientific and social ideas – linked to widespread education – were replacing many of the religious certainties of the past. The document that announced the arrival of this new country was the Declaration of Independence, signed on 4 July 1776 – the date thought of as the birthday of the United States.

The man who wrote most of the declaration was Thomas Jefferson, who went on to become the third US president. For more than two centuries he has been seen as the person who put into words some of the noblest human aims – for equality under the law, and the right to 'life, liberty and the pursuit of happiness'.

Many Americans see Jefferson as a man who sought to pull the state away from any Church. Unlike the country from which America gained its independence, there was no equivalent of the Church of England. But other Americans – hoping that the US will become a more strongly Christian country – look for clues in some of Jefferson's other writing. In 1816, for example, he wrote: 'I have little doubt that the whole country will soon be rallied to the unity of our Creator, and, I hope, to the pure doctrines of Jesus also.'

THE VOTING BOOTH

Democracy and privilege?

Can any government system which allows special privileges to certain religions exist in a country that considers itself to be democratic and representative?

The religious settlements in most European countries date from that turbulent period in the seventeenth century. By the beginning of the eighteenth century, most European countries promised some form of religious freedom, even if one particular denomination was dominant. Even countries with state religions, such as Great Britain, allowed other groups freedom of worship.

Laws that bind

At the heart of any system of government are laws.
These are the rules that governments create and enforce
so that society follows the pattern that its people have
chosen. Laws are an important way of defining a society,
whether it is governed totally or in part through its
religious beliefs (by some form of theocracy), or
whether it professes to keep Church and state separate.

Different approaches
Countries with a Christian tradition generally avoid preserving the
Christian link in their laws. Laws guaranteeing religious freedom
allow Christians and those who belong to other faiths to worship

SEPARATE OR PLAYING A PART?
*Farhan Bhatti, an American Muslim, had this to say about the relationship between Islam and US society in September 2008: 'As Muslims, we do indeed believe that Islam is the best system. But we do not live in a Muslim country, nor do we live in a theocracy. When you have Muslims living in a non-Muslim country, Islam does not preclude Muslims from getting involved in the affairs of that country for the betterment of that society. This is, actually, a form of **da'wah** (an invitation to people to understand Islam) because as more Muslims become involved in society, the misconstrued images and stereotypes that some Americans have in their minds about Muslims will begin to be eradicated.'*

An Orthodox Jew casts his vote in a polling station in an Israeli election in 2009. Orthodox Jews try to apply the laws and codes of sacred writing in their daily lives.

as they please. A **free press** allows Christian preachers to use the media easily and often (see pages 38-41). At a local level, however, some laws reflect a religious influence. For religious reasons it was illegal to sell alcohol on Sundays in parts of Wales well into the twentieth century. Similar restrictions still apply in many counties of the United States. So religious believers in these countries can shape laws on a local level.

Many Muslims, on the other hand, believe that their religion calls for a single, Islamic state that would include all people of that faith. Such a wide-ranging state, called the caliphate, would wipe away many of the national boundaries that exist now. At its heart would be the Islamic set of laws known as **sharia** (see page 24). At present that goal is still an ideal, and Muslims must maintain their beliefs either in a country with a majority-Muslim population (such as Egypt or Indonesia) or as a **minority** in a more diverse society (such as the UK, United States or Australia).

The widespread discussion in many countries about religious laws – and how they relate to the wider country – has led to some surprises. Many British people, for example, fear that any introduction of sharia would threaten the Christian traditions of the country. However, Rowan Williams, Archbishop of Canterbury (and the highest-ranking Anglican **cleric**), has stated that the introduction of some aspects of sharia is 'unavoidable'; otherwise, many British Muslims would find it hard to relate to the British legal system.

FRANCE'S BAN ON THE BURQA

France has a tradition of religious freedom like many western countries. Its national motto, 'Liberty, equality and brotherhood', dates back to the time of the French Revolution in 1789. The political system before the revolution ensured that the Catholic Church had special privileges. Those privileges were abandoned after 1789, and the French were proud to promote and support religious freedom. A law dating back to 1905 calls for French society to be **secular** and no religious clothing can be worn in schools or public places.

But a dispute over one item of clothing has shaken French society, causing people to re-examine the boundaries between Church and state. The dispute spills over into questions of terrorism, racism and the role of women. The piece of clothing is the burqa, an enveloping outer garment which covers nearly all of a woman's body, sometimes including her face.

France has one of the largest Muslim minorities (about seven per cent) in western Europe. Ever since a bitter civil war in Algeria (a Muslim country and former French colony) in the 1990s, the relationship between non-Muslim French people and the immigrant Muslim community has been strained. With the rise of **Islamist** terrorism in other parts of the world, tensions have become more acute.

French politicians are now trying to find a balance between maintaining their secular tradition (some see the burqa as a religious symbol) and the wider issue of religious freedom. In 2003, the French government banned women's headscarves (common in the Muslim community) because they were considered religious symbols. Seven years later it passed a law forbidding people to conceal their face in public places. This law was partly an anti-terrorist measure. Police and security forces need to identify people's faces, but many Muslims viewed it as targeting women in their community.

A French Muslim woman in full burqa is accompanied by a supporter as she makes a symbolic protest outside the French National Assembly in Paris.

THE VOTING BOOTH

Symbols of faith

Do you think that the French ban of the burqa is a justified way of keeping French society free from religious influence, or is it an attack on religious freedom? What about a Christian cross or a Jewish star of David?

Islamic crossroads

Jewish and Christian societies have lived under theocracies briefly during the course of their long histories, but theocracy as a system of government has never taken root permanently. By and large, Jews and Christians accept that their religious and national responsibilities do not overlap. Muslims face different pressures. Many of them are happy to follow the Jewish and Christian examples of separating Church and state on a personal level. Others believe that being a Muslim is the most important thing, and that Islam should underpin everything.

Fundamental differences

Many Christians and Jews feel strongly that their religious beliefs should be the foundation of their countries' laws. But they also see that this goal is probably unrealistic. Instead, they approach secular government in one of two ways. Some groups – such as Amish Christians and Hasidic Jews – remove themselves from society as far as possible or impose strict rules about clothing and behaviour. Others, prompted by television preachers (see pages 38-41) and other believers, hope to introduce their ideas into politics, education and society generally.

Those two approaches allow believers to stay true to their faith while accepting that there are others around them who do not share their faith. They also follow an instruction that Jesus gave: 'Render unto Caesar the things that are Caesar's and unto God the things that are God's.' Most people agree that Jesus was telling his followers that they could obey the rules of a government (even if it is led by non-believers) as long as they were true to their faith on a personal level.

Some Muslims take a different view and believe that they should strive for entirely Muslim societies, in which Islam guides every aspect of people's lives – as well as all society's laws and international behaviour. They look back to the period immediately after the death of Muhammad, the founder of Islam, in the seventh century. Muslims at that time tried to make sure that the moral and legal heart of Islam would survive under the caliphs (successors) of Muhammad.

Islam spread widely across Asia and north Africa and into Europe during the seventh and eighth centuries. Country boundaries (for example, between Algeria and Morocco or Iraq and Iran) mattered very little to Muslims at that time. This was because the people living within the wider Muslim area – known as the caliphate – believed that sharia (Islamic law – see panel) should apply equally and everywhere.

It became difficult for Muslims to build and maintain this unified Islamic nation, so they found themselves living in other kingdoms and countries with national boundaries. But the goal of building a huge, united Muslim nation – a new caliphate – still exists for many Muslims.

Supporters of the Muslim Brotherhood protest about the conduct of Egypt's elections in 2005. The organization was banned at the time, but has since taken power, following the Egyptian revolution of 2011. President Mubarak resigned and Mohamed Morsi of the Brotherhood was then elected president in the country's first democratic elections in 2012.

Sharia law

Islamic law is the 'glue' that holds Muslim communities together and underpins ideas of a caliphate. This code of laws is known as sharia, which is an Arabic word meaning 'the well-worn path to water'. The roots of Islam are in the Arabian desert, so a path to water is a powerful symbol of people's quest for truth and justice. And they believe that Islam provides that 'water', as long as people follow its guidance.

Sharia is a mixture of statements from the Koran (Islam's sacred writing) and the writings of Islamic scholars over the past 15 centuries. The governments that have introduced the most theocratic elements in recent years – Iran, Saudi Arabia and Afghanistan, for example – have based their systems of politics, justice and doing business on sharia.

In some instances, the outside world views sharia justice as primitive, and even barbaric. Punishments in some countries include cutting hands off or stoning people to death. Taken as a whole, sharia offers believers a merciful way of living together. Religious leaders from other faiths have recognized this special role of sharia. Dr Rowan Williams, Archbishop of Canterbury and the most senior figure in the Church of England, points out that sharia is often misunderstood by outsiders and that it has a long tradition of inspiring Muslims as well as people beyond the Islamic community.

An Indonesian sharia official canes a woman as a punishment for having a relationship with a man who was not her husband. Many non-Muslims find such punishments barbaric.

Political specialists use the word Islamism to describe this form of political Islam, and Islamist to describe someone who promotes it. Islamism lies at the heart of many disputes within and between Muslim countries – and some terrorists even use it to justify violence against non-Muslims.

The widespread protests in many Muslim countries through 2011 – known collectively as the Arab Spring – have highlighted the issue of Islamism. Protesters joyfully overthrew dictators and have pressed for greater democracy. In several of those countries, though, the most powerful political groups hold Islamist views – and could have great influence after elections are held.

VOICE OF THE PEOPLE

FEAR AND SADNESS

The Taliban are a group of Islamists who held power in Afghanistan during the 1990s and who hope to regain control there. They followed a chilling interpretation of sharia law, with public executions and strict control of the people (especially women). Some people fear that the democratic uprisings of the Arab Spring could encourage more such brutal governments.

*The following comment on Reuters news agency website, days after Colonel Gaddafi's capture and execution in Libya, typifies those fears: 'This is all very sad. Everything about the uprising and the government's attempts to stop it. Before the uprising, Gaddafi was a moderate leader as far as Arab leaders go. Should we be concerned that the uprisings (Arab Spring) will bring in radicals who will align with other radicals as they pursue a **totalitarian** way of life? Yes. Already, the Christians in Egypt have suffered great death and deprivation at the hands of the freedom fighters. A goal of the radicals is to unite the Arab world under one caliphate and restore a global Muslim rule. I am concerned.'*

A lasting legacy

A government does more than decide on rules and regulations for its people. It builds ways of thinking, which linger – sometimes as dim memories, sometimes in people's attitudes – well beyond the lifetime of that government. Whole nations, it seems, retain memories in the same way that individuals do.

VOICE OF THE PEOPLE

'A PEOPLE OF GOD'
Cotton Mather was a Puritan minister and author who lived in Massachusetts during the seventeenth and eighteenth centuries. In 1692 he wrote about the special nature of his fellow New Englanders: 'The New Englanders are a People of God settled in those which were once the Devil's Territories, and it may easily be supposed that the Devil was exceedingly disturbed when he perceived such a People here accomplishing the Promise of old made unto our Blessed Jesus, That He should have the Utmost parts of the Earth for his possession.'

Roger Williams, the Baptist preacher and founder of Rhode Island, is one of the international figures honoured by the Reformation Monument in Geneva, Switzerland.

English people, for example, retained enough happy memories of monarchy to welcome Charles II back to rule them 21 years after they had executed his father, King Charles I. The French did not lose their taste for independence and democracy while their country was controlled by the Germans during the **Second World War**. Some political observers look at the harsh laws in modern Russia and conclude that Russian people expect strictness after centuries of absolute monarchy and then communism.

Echoes of the past

Theocracy has a similar effect on people's thinking. Elements of life under a theocracy remain long after the system of government has been abandoned by a community. These could be called folk memories and they pop up in unlikely forms. In the American state of Massachusetts, for example, diners can stop for lunch at the Pilgrim Café. They might wear Puritan brand sports shirts or Mayflower brand tennis shoes. All these names refer back to the seventeenth century when the first English settlers (the Pilgrims) arrived on the ship the *Mayflower*. They formed a theocracy guided by strict Protestant (Puritan) beliefs.

The company names are harmless – and sometimes amusing – reminders of the past, and have no real connection to the modern world. Or do they? Until 2004 – more than three centuries after the Puritan theocracy ended – people in Massachusetts could not buy alcoholic drinks at off-licences on a Sunday. The Sunday ban still applies in neighbouring Connecticut. The 'no alcohol sales on Sunday' laws in both states reflect the opinion of seventeenth-century lawmakers (when both states were theocracies). Even in the twenty-first century, some of that original thinking seems to hold true.

Apparently outdated regulations dating from stricter religious periods are known as blue laws. Some seem absurd to modern people (see panel right), but the laws remain, even if they have not been enforced for many, many years.

Occasionally, people who have no religious beliefs argue in favour of such laws. One example is the continuing debate about Sunday trading in the UK. Until very recently, the only shops that were permitted to open on Sundays were corner shops and some newsagents. Like the New England blue laws, the restrictions dated back to a time when religious thinking lay behind law-making. Many people argued that Sundays might be the only day when workers could shop – if they worked on other days. Gradually the British government allowed more and more freedom for all sorts of shops to open. Some of the strongest opposition to the changes came not from religious leaders, but from trades unions. They argued that keeping Sundays special guaranteed that workers would have a chance to rest after a busy working week.

Even if people today don't pay much attention to blue laws and other relics of a more religious past, their attitudes can reflect the values that led to those laws. The United States is a good example. Compared with similar countries in the western world, the American government offers few automatic benefits to its citizens. Americans have to pay for their medical care and receive far less government support when they are unwell or out of work.

Most Americans believe that their system is normal, and that Europeans are lazy or misguided to expect more support from their governments. One major reason for this difference in attitudes can be traced to America's religious history. Its most influential European settlers in the seventeenth century were English Puritans, who valued self-reliance and hard work. Their values linger in the US, where people believe that they are responsible for their own actions – and expect far less outside help if things go wrong.

Americans in many states have to hide open bottles of alcohol inside brown paper bags if they want to drink in public. This is a legacy of the anti-alcohol attitudes of the seventeenth-century Puritans who controlled those areas.

BLUE LAWS

Rules and regulations that once echoed strongly-held religious views, but which no longer apply to the modern world, are called blue laws. Most of them remain unchanged but ignored among the other laws of a county, state or country. Why? Governments fear that if they begin to get rid of dozens of laws because they are outdated or ridiculous, people might question whether other laws could be safely ignored.

Below are some of the most absurd examples of blue laws that still exist (even though they are not enforced):
• It is illegal to wear a false moustache if it causes laughter in a church (Alabama, US)
• A man may not kiss his wife on a Sunday (City of Hartford, Connecticut, US)
• It is illegal to walk a cow down Main Street after 1pm on a Sunday (City of Little Rock, Arkansas, US)
• Households will be fined if they keep Christmas decorations up after 14 January (Maine, US)
• It is illegal to eat peanuts in church (Massachusetts, US)
• A husband may beat his wife as long as he does so in public, on a Sunday, and on the courthouse steps (Huntington, West Virginia, US)
• It is an offence to hang clothes out to dry on a Sunday (Switzerland)

Are blue laws a bad thing?
Which of the following views do you agree with?
YES: they're ridiculous and have no place in the modern world
NO: they're harmless and besides, once people start realizing some (unenforced) laws are silly, they might lose respect for other laws

In God we trust?

A society of believers might think it would be easy to base a government on religious principles. But if you think a bit further, the picture becomes less clear-cut. Will the government be Christian? If so, which of the thousands of Christian denominations should be the one to rule? Or will the government be Jewish? People who think of themselves as Jewish can follow one of several traditions of religious practice – and many Jews consider themselves to be part of an ethnic group rather than a denomination. Muslims follow traditions such as Shi'a or Sunni, and there can be hostility between those groups.

THE PLEDGE OF ALLEGIANCE

'I pledge **allegiance** to the flag of the United States of America, and to the republic for which it stands, one nation under God, indivisible, with liberty and justice for all.'

American children have been reciting the Pledge of Allegiance since 1892 as a mark of loyalty to their country (with the flag as its symbol). But at the start of the Cold War in the late 1940s, many Americans wanted to contrast their country with their enemy – the Soviet Union, which was atheist under communism. This is why the words 'under God' were added to the American pledge in 1954. Those two words have divided Americans ever since, into those who feel they capture national opinion and those who believe that their country should not have an established (state) religion.

A group of young American schoolchildren pledge allegiance to the US flag, as they do at the start of every school day. How many of them know about the dispute surrounding the words 'under God', which they will recite?

Deep rifts

Disputes and lingering disagreements have a way of creeping into most religions. Christianity was more or less united for the first few centuries of its existence, but now it is hard to calculate precisely how many separate denominations describe themselves as Christian. The figure might be 15,000, 20,000 or even 35,000. Jews also find themselves divided into categories (Liberal, Orthodox, Reform) depending on their interpretation of Biblical laws.

Even Islam, the faith that has come closest to producing lasting theocracy, has its share of sharp divisions. Muslims look back to a time when, led by the Prophet Muhammad, they agreed how to put the words of the Koran into practice. The principal division within Islam – between its Shi'a and Sunni branches – goes back to the years following Muhammad's death. Disputes arose about who should be the prophet's rightful successor and which form of religious practice should govern Islam. Today's news reports about terrorist attacks and suicide bombers can often be traced back to the same Shi'a-Sunni split.

The Shi'a-Sunni rift is a huge obstacle to Muslims forming a single, united Islamic country, or caliphate. Which tradition would Islamic judges follow in deciding on divorces, robbery or murder? Would members of the other tradition abide by such a decision? Similar splits and religious rivalries spelled the end of Christian theocracies in fifteenth-century Florence (with its Catholic theocracy), sixteenth-century Geneva (Calvinist Protestant) and seventeenth-century Massachusetts (Puritan Protestant).

Fearing theocracy

Another source of unease is the relationship between religious and secular forces in many countries. Countries with clear guidelines about separating Church and state often have large numbers of religious believers within their borders. Conflict arises when secularists fear that religious beliefs are gaining too much influence. These fears can be reversed when believers accuse 'godless' people of restricting their religious freedom.

India, the world's second-largest country in terms of population, is sometimes the setting for religious disputes of the most violent kind. It is the largest country in what was once a colony known as British India. When Britain granted the region independence in 1947, it divided the colony along religious lines. Many faiths are represented in the area, but the main two are Hindu and Muslim.

Hindus and Muslims lived together under British rule, but problems arose as the British prepared to grant independence to the region. Hindus make up the majority in much of the Indian peninsula, and Muslims are the larger group to the east and west. So the British divided India into the country known as India (the Hindu centre) and the Muslim-dominated Pakistan to the east and west. East Pakistan became known as Bangladesh in the 1970s.

Modern India may have a mainly Hindu population, but its constitution grants freedom to Muslims, Christians and members of other faiths. Some fundamentalist Hindus, however, object to the presence of these 'foreign' faiths. Violence has sometimes erupted in areas where these religious groups live near each other.

The United States is a country with clear guidelines, or so it seems. On one hand, it has a constitution that prohibits any form of state religion. On the other, it has one of the highest church-going populations in the industrialized world. The two forces often seem to be on a collision course.

The National Day of Prayer

Since 1952, US presidents have issued a proclamation that a certain day (usually the first Thursday in May) should be a National Day of Prayer. The idea seems harmless, and President Obama has carried on the tradition. But opponents say that setting aside a day for the purpose of praying is introducing theocracy into what should be a secular society. They refer to the First Amendment to the US Constitution, which says that there: 'should be no law respecting the establishing of a religion, or prohibiting the free exercise thereof.'

Do you think that having a national day of prayer establishes a religion, or do you feel that protests are going too far?

A Hindu monk offers up a prayer on the banks of the River Ganges, which is sacred to India's Hindus. Some members of the Hindu community go beyond traditional ceremonies and attack their non-Hindu neighbours.

End of the line

Theocracies tend to fade into more common forms of government such as monarchy, democracy or even dictatorship. Some of the reasons for this are usually apparent from the start. Even in a society that shares most fundamental beliefs, disagreements can threaten a theocratic government. It is hard for people to agree on the right religious formula to transform politics – and harder still to stay true to a formula when the government faces a range of non-religious problems every day.

Politics as usual?

It is easy to concentrate on the religious nature of theocracies. People inside those countries and observers on the outside can identify many of the elements that relate to religious rule – the harsh punishments, the control of the media (see pages 38-41)

VOICE OF THE PEOPLE

LEAVING THE AMISH

Saloma Furlong is the author of Why I Left the Amish, *an account of her childhood in a strict Amish community in the US state of Ohio. Most Amish people are descendants of Protestants from Germany and Switzerland who fled to America in the eighteenth century to avoid religious persecution. They believe that much of the modern world is corrupt and that they can only be true Christians by keeping themselves separate from American society as much as possible.*

*Within their separate communities, the Amish live according to religious and social (almost political) customs. Much social and political Amish life centres on working together as a community. If one family loses a barn in a fire, the rest of the community joins together to build a new one. Saloma Furlong found this side of Amish life hardest to leave, when she did go. She explains her mixed feelings: 'If the Amish way of life could be separated from the religion, I may still be living their lifestyle. But I found the religion to be a **punitive** one that embraces the pain of life more than it does the joy of life. Perhaps this is left over from the days when our ancestors endured persecution for their religious beliefs. The way this plays out in the religion is that there is more focus on wrongdoers than on the people who are upstanding members of the community.'*

Members of an Amish community in Pennsylvania make their way to a church service. The Amish try to avoid contact with most aspects of the modern world such as electricity and cars.

and the sober atmosphere overall. But political experts remind us that theocracies are forms of government, and that they should really be seen as the result of extreme political activity.

The most extreme political activity is a revolution, the violent overthrow of one type of government by supporters of another system. The French Revolution violently replaced a monarchy with a republic; the Russian Revolution replaced a monarchy with a communist system. The government of modern Iran, which many people describe as a theocracy, arose out of the 1979 revolution, which overthrew the Iranian monarchy.

Revolutions, however, often lose some of their extremism after the initial period of violent change. French revolutionaries, once in power, turned on each other as they tried to be more revolutionary than each other.

Eventually, they compromised by allowing a military leader (Napoleon Bonaparte) take power. Some modern observers look for signs that Islamic revolutionaries are willing to compromise in Iran.

Surviving evidence

Many people are not aware that some of the societies most famous for being theocracies were, in fact, other types of government with strong religious influences. Sixteenth-century Geneva at the time of John Calvin (see page 13) had strict laws governing church attendance, which aimed to keep Sunday sacred and restrict what people could say or do in public. But the people who made and enforced these laws were not Protestant ministers: they were officials elected in the same way as representatives of Geneva's government for many decades. They were heavily influenced by Calvin and his followers, but the mechanics of government remained the same.

The mechanics of government survived Calvin, although his influence has never vanished from Geneva. Compared with areas of Switzerland that remained Catholic throughout the sixteenth century, Geneva retains a serious, sober atmosphere. If the strong (some say theocratic) Islamic influence on Iran and Saudi Arabia were to fade in the future, the surviving republic (Iran) and monarchy (Saudi Arabia) would no doubt include examples of Islamic thinking.

Faith communities

Other large groups that run along theocratic lines, but are not really governments, pose different problems. Such faith communities include many religious groups that set themselves apart from wider society. These distinctions can take the form of:
• distinctive clothing (as worn, for example, by Hasidic Jews, Rastafarians and the Amish),
• language (the Amish again),
• rules about food and drink (Mormons),
• medicine (Christian Scientists).

In these communities the mix of religion and politics is weighted towards religion so they are less concerned with taxation, foreign policy, roads and most of the practical matters that occupy much of a government's time and energy. In their own way, however, these groups can influence their members as strongly as other types of government.

WHEN IT ALL GOES WRONG

Faith communities, run like theocracies, can sometimes descend into chaos. One extreme example was the end of Jonestown in 1978. During the mid-1950s, a young man named Jim Jones founded the Peoples Temple Christian Church Full Gospel in the US state of Indiana. The Temple, as it was known, aimed to promote racial and social equality.

Jones moved the Temple to California in the 1960s, continuing to attract people of all races to the Temple and helping the local poor and homeless. By the 1970s, though, Jones had become convinced that the US government and other organizations were targeting the Temple. He became suspicious of those around him, accusing some of being traitors to the Temple. Meanwhile he continued to preach a mixture of Christianity and socialism.

By 1977, newspapers began investigating claims that Jones and his Temple operated as a cult, forcing members to do many things against their will and in fear of their lives. Jones and hundreds of his followers fled to a community they had built (Jonestown) in the rainforest of Guyana in South America. The media stories continued and in November 1978 an investigating group from the US Congress flew to Guyana to check on reports about Jonestown. Although the group viewed Jonestown favourably, Jones believed that the end was near. On 18 November 1978, he assembled members of the community by a public hall, where people lined up to drink a purple mixture that contained deadly poison. Within minutes, more than 900 people had died.

American actor Powers Boothe portrayed Jim Jones in a TV movie which re-enacted the terrifying events in Jonestown in November 1978.

The media and theocracy

Rebels surround a capital city with the aim of overthrowing an unpopular dictator. Government forces have more weapons and ammunition, backed up by patrol helicopters with searchlights and fast-moving troop carriers. The odds against rebel success are poor, but they feel they have one weapon that could be decisive – public opinion. If they can let people know that the dictator's end might be in sight, their forces would swell. The question is: how can they get their message to the people?

Many countries have experienced these events, and very often rebels have succeeded in using public opinion to turn the tables on a hated ruler. For the rebels the first step towards achieving success is often capturing a radio or television broadcasting centre. Rebels might even announce victory (without having fired a shot), knowing that people will come and help them round up security forces and other hated symbols of an oppressive regime.

Knowledge is power

Scenes like that have played out many times, with small armed groups achieving their aims because they were able to control the flow of information. Equally, unpopular governments remain in power by using **propaganda** which attempts either to convince people that the government is legitimate, or that is powerful enough to crush any opposition. Propaganda played a part during the communist era in Europe, when communist governments frequently broadcast images of their fighting forces and weapons.

Why discuss rebel groups and dictators when studying theocracy? The answer is contained in a simple sentence that has been repeated for centuries: 'Knowledge is power.' A dictator can spread information (or knowledge) as propaganda, and a rebel group can use it to spark an uprising, so the flow of information plays a hugely important role in the area where religion and politics mix.

A man relaxes by watching golf on TV in Dubai. Some people fear that Dubai and some of its Middle East neighbours might bow to religious pressure over what they should broadcast.

We use the word 'media' to describe a wide range of methods of communication which spread ideas. Nowadays the media include not just examples of the written word (books, newspapers and magazines) but also radio, television, mobile phones and the Internet. Most people agree that the free flow of information by these means provides one of the best defences of democracy. People can find out all sides of an argument and make up their minds what they think.

No one seriously believes that the UK, US, Australia or any other country with a free press is likely to become a theocracy. But the freedom these countries enjoy – especially the unregulated freedom of access offered by the Internet – allows people with strongly held religious views to transmit their message. These people want to shape national laws so that they reflect their own religious views. The most extreme examples are America's 'televangelists' who broadcast on both radio and

TELEVANGELISTS AND POLITICS

A government often uses the media to further its own ends. In some Islamic countries, such as Iran and Saudi Arabia (which are very theocratic), close control of the media ensures that the approved religious message gets through. Non-theocratic countries, though, also have a tradition of religious broadcasting. In recent years, many religious broadcasters have tried to influence elections – and by extension, the way in which countries are governed.

The most extreme examples are in the US, which has a tradition of huge crowds gathering to hear preachers (who are almost always Protestant). The formal word for someone who spreads the gospel is an evangelist. Many evangelists understand the potential of television to spread their message beyond the thousands they might address in a crowd, to the millions who watch TV. Some televangelists express strong opinions about the political issues that are debated during campaigning for national elections. Critics see them as upsetting the delicate balance between Church and state, but supporters see no problem with this.

television (see panel above). This falls short of true theocracy, but a political system could be nudged in a particular direction by such influences and the Internet is crowded with people eager to mix religion and politics.

Controlling the flow

Just what happens – or what could happen – in a theocracy to control the flow of information? Can a government really try to stop the flow of ideas? The answer is yes, although the position is changing. All forms of strong government, whether they are dictatorships, communist regimes or religious-influenced systems, want to promote the appearance of unity in their country.

When most of a country's people hold similar core beliefs, it is easier for a government in a theocracy to control what people can and should be able to read or watch. After all, who would want to face the charge that they were promoting evil religious views in what they wanted to read or write, or watch? A theocracy, like any other form of government, must meet the basic needs of its people – for food, shelter, education and housing – and it can expect protests if it fails to do so. But a theocratic government has a ready response if it is accused of manipulating information: we are only trying to protect the people from bad ways of thinking.

Leading Protestant preacher Eddie Villanueva has twice been a presidential candidate in the Philippines. His huge political rallies resemble enthusiastic religious meetings.

THE VOTING BOOTH

Controlling what people see and hear?

In countries that cherish freedom of worship, what sort of limits should be placed on the spread of religious ideas? Should there be complete freedom? Should religion be kept in a church or temple, rather than on the television and in newspapers? Or is a decent compromise possible between informing the public about religion and forcing religious views on them?

Looking ahead

Predicting the future, in the area of international politics, is very tricky. It is easy to draw conclusions from recent evidence and get things completely wrong. Some trends seem to go in one direction, only to peter out for unexpected reasons. Equally, hidden currents of public opinion may go unnoticed by political experts for some time, and then burst on the scene suddenly.

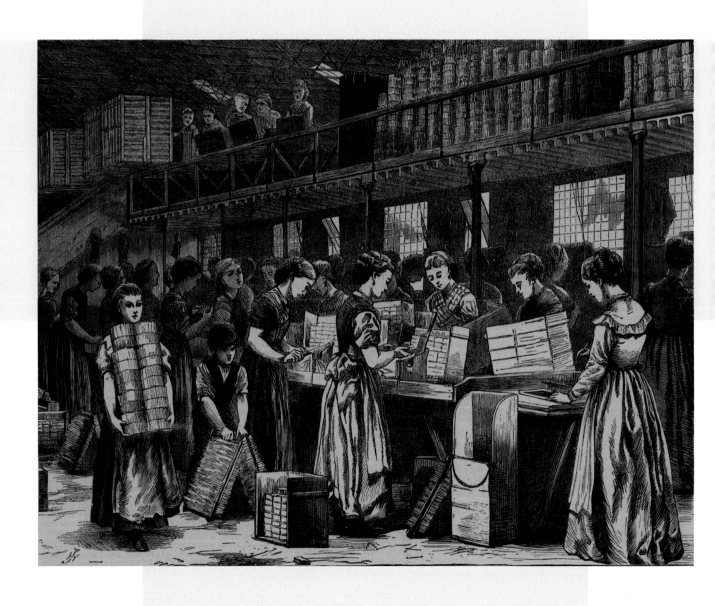

One expert prediction made by the founders of communism, Karl Marx and Friedrich Engels, turned out to be completely wrong. Both believed that the first communist governments would be formed in Britain and Germany in the late nineteenth century. Why? Because they thought a communist revolutionwould take place in a country with highly developed factories. Instead, communism first took root in one of the world's least industrialized countries, Russia.

Similarly, few political experts today had foreseen the growing sense of dissatisfaction of people in the Middle East, who live in some of the most strictly controlled countries in the world. Yet there a wave of protests has swept leaders from power and threatened others across north Africa and the Middle East in what has become known as the Arab Spring (see The Voting Booth).

Young women working in crowded conditions in a London match factory in 1871. Britain's hundreds of factories led Karl Marx to predict that the first communist revolution would take place either there or in equally industrial Germany.

The way of the future?

What place does theocracy have in predictions for the twenty-first century? Most people believe that the age of theocracies is over, and the stage is set for more democracies, dictatorships and perhaps even modified monarchies. That dismissal of theocracy is probably wrong for a number of reasons.

First, it is never a good idea for a historian to rule something out – it will probably happen. Second, it is possible that some forms of theocracy just might thrive in the future and there is evidence for this, based on religious basics – fundamentalism, in fact. We know that 'back to basics' fundamentalism gains ground when people feel threatened by the pace of change. Many people across the world feel just such a threat now, with issues such as terrorism, economic hardship and environmental problems occupying people's minds.

This reaction to sudden changes is nothing new. The pace of change – with new forms of communication, especially – can be overwhelming, and many people fear that greedy people will benefit at the expense of the deserving. Many young people have organized protests to help promote fairer societies along with a more sensible use of the world's resources, such as oil. This sort of involvement is sometimes considered left-wing because the people want their governments to play a bigger

The slogan on the Occupy London banner in late 2011 shows how religion has once again crept into the world of politics. Protesters had originally intended to camp in the heart of London's financial centre. Instead, they found space (and some support) just outside St Paul's Cathedral.

part in solving major problems. But the same modern problems that lead some people to left-wing protest send others back to the core of their religious faith.

Many young people – whether they be Christians, Muslims, Jews, Hindus or Buddhists – are turning to strict interpretations of their faiths as a way of finding certainty in an uncertain world. This religious change has also produced change in the world of politics. Some Muslim countries are considering following Iran's example, and allowing their religious leaders to influence the law-making process. Christian preachers in the US and across the western world continue to urge their followers to support certain political causes and candidates. Religious values seem to be a powerful force in many countries today.

One area in which religious views seem to be making a comeback is as part of the wave of 'Occupy' protests that sprang up in cities around

More theocracy?

The pro-democracy uprisings of 2011 in many Muslim countries – including Tunisia, Libya, Egypt, Syria and Bahrain – have become known as the Arab Spring. The name has arisen for two reasons. The first is that these protests began early in the year (during the spring). The second – and for many observers, the more important – reason is that the protesters were calling for an end to strict repression and were in favour of more social freedom. So the protests were like seedlings in the spring that would soon blossom (into democracy).

Some observers fear that the protests might simply replace one sort of dictatorship with another, religious-based dictatorship. They look back at the 1979 revolution in Iran, which swept an unpopular leader (the shah) from power but replaced him with a strict Islamic theocracy. In October 2011, ten months after Hosni Mubarak was swept from power in Egypt, Muslims and Coptic Christians clashed in bitter riots, leaving 28 Copts dead. However, Egyptians elected an Islamic president in 2012, Mohamed Morsi of the Muslim Brotherhood.

Do you think that such fears are understandable – in Egypt and throughout the countries of the Arab Spring – or will people of all faiths feel a part of these new societies?

the world in late 2011. Tent cities sprang up in public squares and plazas, often near financial centres such as Wall Street in New York and the City of London. The protesters represented a broad range of views – not all agreed on what to do, but they believed that the international financial system was at fault.

Ten or twenty years before, such protests were linked by left-wing protests and the slogans on posters were about jobs and workers and money. Those themes were all on display in 2011 as well. But at least one banner in the Occupy London camp by St Paul's Cathedral in the City of London had a different message: 'What would Jesus do?'

Glossary

accomplice   Someone who helps plan or perform a criminal act, and who must be punished for it along with the criminal.

allegiance   Loyalty and devotion (to something or to an ideal).

Buddhism   A world religion that developed in India about 2,500 years ago.

city-state   A city and the surrounding area that makes its own laws, much as a country does.

cleric   A person with special training who has responsibilities and an official role within an organized religion.

communism   A political system in which all property is owned by the community. A communist government provides work, health care, education and housing, but may deny people certain freedoms.

compromise   An agreement between two groups that involves each side giving in a little, in order to find common ground.

constitution   A written document that spells out the aims and basic principles of an organization or a political group – or even a country.

da'wah   Preaching Islam, and especially helping non-Muslims understand more about it.

democracy   A form of government in which all, or most of the people have a say in choosing their leaders.

denomination   A branch of a larger religion; members of a denomination share common traditions.

dictatorship   A form of government in which a single person has complete control and absolute power.

dissent   Political opposition to a government's policies.

Enlightenment   Also known as the Age of Enlightenment, a period during the eighteenth century when European thinkers tried to change society through advances in science and learning.

free press   Media (such as newspapers, magazines, television and radio) that are free from government control.

fundamentalism   A belief in going back to the basic, core values (the fundamentals) of a religion – especially in response to the modern world.

heretic   Someone who proposes beliefs that are different from a religious group's established set of beliefs.

Islam   A world religion that developed in Arabia in the seventh century; its members, Muslims, believe that its founder, the Prophet Muhammad, received the word of God directly and wrote it in the sacred Koran.

Islamist   Someone who believes that Islam is not simply a religion, but also a set of political beliefs.

minority   A group that makes up less than half of a larger group.

monarchy   A system of government in which the leader, or national symbol, remains in power for life, and is replaced by his or her child.

Mormon A member of the Church of Jesus Christ of Latter-day Saints, which believes in the Christian Bible as well as the Book of Mormon (a set of sacred writings believed to have been dictated by an angel to Joseph Smith in the nineteenth century).

polygamy Having more than one wife or husband.

propaganda The spreading of news, rumour and sometimes lies to gain political support or to hurt the reputation of those who oppose you.

Protestant A Christian movement that opposed the power of the Catholic church in the sixteenth century.

punitive Intended as a harsh punishment.

Puritan A member of a Protestant movement in the sixteenth and seventeenth centuries, which wanted to rid (purify) the Church of England of practices that were not mentioned in the Bible.

revolution Forcibly overthrowing a government and replacing it with another.

Second World War The war which began in Europe and spread around the world between 1939 and 1945.

secular Separate from, or having nothing to do with, religion.

sharia A set of codes and laws that guides the moral and religious behaviour of Muslims.

Taliban An Islamist group that ruled much of Afghanistan in the late 1990s and is trying to regain power.

territory (in American history) A region of North America settled by people who want to become part of the United States; a territory needs to pass several tests before it can be admitted to the US as a state.

totalitarian Describes a political system in which the government accepts no limits to its powers, and tries to control every aspect of its people's lives.

Books

Religious Freedom (Campaigns for Change) Sean Connolly (Smart Apple Media, 2005)
What is a Theocracy? R. Miller (Crabtree, 2011)
Fundamentalism Alex Woolf (Wayland, 2003)

Websites

Religions of the World
http://www.42explore2.com/religion.htm

Religion Online
http://library.thinkquest.org/26756/

United Nations Cyberschoolbus
cyberschoolbus.un.org/

Index